W9-BKS-311

MEXICAN
LOW-FAT COOKING

COLE GROUP

FOOD AND FIESTA

*I*n Mexico good cooking is a celebration, a
mystical union of food and *fiesta* that
ministers to the deepest human needs to be
not simply fed but nourished. Combining
enlightened recipes and low-fat cooking
techniques with colorful, festive Mexican fare
that nourishes both body and soul, this book
celebrates the delicious fusion of cooking and
culture that is *la cocina mexicana*.

THE MEXICAN CULINARY TRADITION

With a history of good cooking that predates the discovery of the New World, Mexico has influenced the way the entire world cooks and eats. Many of our most familiar and favorite foods—avocados, beans of all kinds, corn, chocolate, peanuts, pineapple, potatoes, pumpkins, squash, sunflowers, sweet potatoes, tomatoes, turkey, even vanilla—are native to Mexico. No wonder Mexican cuisine remains among the most appreciated of all international culinary traditions.

The foods used in the cuisine of Mexico are simple and inexpensive, but without them no Mexican dish is truly authentic. Depending on where you live, you can find most of the following ingredients at supermarkets, farmers' markets, and specialty food shops:

*Beans—frijoles—*especially pintos and black (or turtle) beans, are daily fare in the Mexican diet. Although few vegetables in Mexican cooking are served unadorned, beans are traditionally served plain—directly from the pot *(frijoles de olla)*, or mashed and cooked into a thick paste *(frijoles refritos)*. According to Mexican culinary tradition, chiles and certain herbs (epazote, Mexican oregano, mint, cumin, rosemary, and anise) help reduce the intestinal flatulence associated with eating beans.

Chiles, the starting point for many Mexican dishes, fall into two broad categories: *Cooking chiles* and *garnish (condiment) chiles.* Cooking varieties are generally mild-flavored and include fresh Anaheim (New Mexico) and poblano chiles, and dried ancho chiles. Garnish (condiment) varieties are hot—hot enough to induce tears, shortness of breath, and a state of ecstatic panic in the uninitiated. These include fresh jalapeño and serrano chiles, and smoke-dried chipotle chiles. Garnish chiles are also available pickled *(en escabeche)*. The hottest parts of any hot chile are the ribs (veins) and, to a lesser extent, the seeds; discard these parts for a milder taste.

Cilantro, also known as Chinese parsley or fresh coriander, has a distinctive flavor that complements chiles. Use it sparingly until you know you are certain you like the taste. Some of the recipes in this book call for fresh cilantro; others specify coriander seeds. Use whichever the recipe specifies, since the flavors are entirely different.

Mexican oregano, a name given to any of several plants used fresh or dried in Mexican cooking, most often refers to the leaves of a small shrub of the *Verbena* family. This herb is more aromatic and pungent than *Origanum,* the "oregano" commonly used in the United States.

Tomatillos, also known as husk tomatoes or ground cherries, have a lemony flavor that intensifies during cooking. Some traditional recipes call for preparing the tomatillos by first removing the papery husks and toasting the tomatillos in a comal (griddle) or ungreased dry skillet until the skins are charred. Uncooked tomatillos are sometimes used as a garnish.

Tortillas made from the corn dough known as *masa* are a mainstay of Mexican cooking, although flour tortillas are popular in Mexico's northern wheat-growing region and in the southwestern U.S. Look for fat-free or reduced-fat tortillas made with oil, not lard.

Along with the use of authentic ingredients, Mexican cuisine emphasizes preparing them carefully to bring out subtleties of flavor and texture that might otherwise be missed. Care in preparation ensures that every ingredient will contribute its best to the dish in process. For example, using puréed raw garlic in a recipe such as Salsa de Chipotle (see page 18) gives a powerful garlicky "bite" to the finished dish. For a milder taste, the garlic is toasted before being puréed. But for Salsa de Jalapeños Rojos (see page 17), the garlic is lightly sautéed and then discarded; only the garlic-tinged cooking oil is used in the final dish.

The best Mexican cooks dispense herbs, spices, and other seasonings with a light hand, using them to highlight the natural flavors of other foods. For example, a classic Mexican herb/spice combination used in the traditional pork dish known as Adobo (see page 64) uses four parts dried Mexican oregano to two parts cumin and one part cloves. This carefully developed formula preserves the balance of flavors in the dish without adding a strong "seasoned" taste. It is this sort of simple yet thoughtful preparation that makes for authentic Mexican cuisine.

¡GOCEN MUCHO!

Guacamole, tacos, enchiladas, burritos, fajitas, chili—you don't have to sacrifice the fun of eating your favorite Mexican foods just because you're cutting down on dietary fat, cholesterol, and calories. The recipes and cooking techniques featured in *Low-Fat Mexican Cooking* are designed for delicious, authentic-tasting Mexican dining that won't undermine your commitment to healthy nutrition.

Specifically, the recipes and ingredients in this book are compatible with current dietary recommendations urging a reduction in dietary fat levels to approximately 30 percent or less of the *total* daily caloric intake. For example, except where otherwise specified, recipes in this book use skim (nonfat) milk, low-fat and part skim cheeses, defatted stock, and other ingredients that help reduce fat intake. Listed at the end of each recipe is nutritional data (number of calories and the amount of fat, percentage of calories from fat, and cholesterol contained in the serving size indicated). The nutritional values do not include optional ingredients and inexact quantities of foods used for garnishing.

As you experience the magical union of good food and fun that is Mexican cooking at its best, remember this important advice: ¡Gocen mucho! ("Enjoy yourselves!")

RECIPES AND TECHNIQUES FOR LOW-FAT MEXICAN COOKING

*T*o health-conscious cooks everywhere who love preparing and eating good Mexican food this book proclaims "¡buen apetito!" From traditional dishes like Pico de Gallo (see page 22) or Adobo (see page 64) to resort specialties such as Enchiladas Verdes de Mariscos (see page 45) or Margarita Sorbet (see page 88), this unique collection of 50 recipes and helpful techniques presents a fiesta of low-fat fare.

APPETIZERS, SOUPS, AND SALADS

Cool and creamy Guacamole with Crudités (see page 16), light but satisfying Sopa de Pollo (see page 34), colorful, cactus-spiked Ensalada de Noche Buena (see page 37)... The recipes in this section offer delicious ways to spice up an hors d'oeuvre tray or perk up a meal with a modicum of fat, cholesterol, and calories.

STUFFED CHILES MONTERREY

Delicious as an appetizer or light luncheon dish, these chiles are filled with a vegetarian stuffing.

12	fresh Anaheim chiles	12
2 tsp	olive oil	2 tsp
¼ cup	dry sherry	60 ml
½ cup	minced onion	125 ml
½ cup	minced mushroom caps	125 ml
4 cups	chopped spinach leaves	900 ml
½ cup	grated mozzarella cheese, part skim milk	125 ml
1 cup	grated low-fat Colby or jack cheese	250 ml
2 cups	bread crumbs, coarsely ground	500 ml
½ tsp	ground cumin	½ tsp
¼ tsp	cayenne pepper	¼ tsp
to taste	salt	to taste

1. Preheat oven to 400°F (205°C). Leaving stems on chiles, slit lengthwise and remove seeds and white membrane. Place chiles, cut side up, in baking dish coated with 1 teaspoon of the oil.

2. In a medium skillet heat sherry and remaining oil until mixture simmers. Add onion and cook over medium-high heat, stirring until onion begins to brown slightly. Add mushrooms and cover; lower heat and cook until mushrooms exude moisture. (Add a teaspoon or so of water if necessary to prevent mushrooms from sticking.) Add spinach. Cover and cook until spinach is wilted (about 3 minutes).

3. Remove from heat and add remaining ingredients; mix well. Stuff chiles with mushroom mixture.

4. Bake until chiles are soft and cheeses have melted (about 30 minutes). Serve hot.

Makes 12 chiles, 6 servings.
Each serving: cal 340, fat 7 g, cal from fat 18%, chol 9 mg

SPICY CRABMEAT TOSTADAS

Great for a quick meal, these light, healthy tostadas are baked rather than deep-fried. Make the filling ahead and top the tostadas right before serving.

¼ cup	minced red onion	60 ml
1 tsp	olive oil	1 tsp
½ tsp	minced garlic	½ tsp
1 cup	diced tomatoes	250 ml
2 tbl	minced cilantro (coriander leaves)	2 tbl
2 cups	cooked crabmeat, shredded	500 ml
6	corn tortillas	6
2 tbl	lemon juice	2 tbl
¼ cup	chopped green bell pepper	60 ml
¼ cup	peeled and chopped cucumber	60 ml
1 cup	shredded lettuce	250 ml
as needed	fresh or bottled salsa	as needed

1. Preheat oven to 350°F (175°C). In a large skillet over medium-high heat, sauté onion in oil until soft (about 3 minutes). Add garlic, tomatoes, cilantro, and crabmeat. Cook for 5 minutes.

2. To prepare tostadas, bake tortillas in a single layer in preheated oven until crisp (about 7–10 minutes). Remove from oven and set aside. In a large bowl mix together lemon juice, bell pepper, cucumber, and lettuce. Divide lettuce mixture among tostadas, then top with crab mixture, and salsa. Serve at once.

Serves 6.
Each serving: cal 115, fat 2 g, cal from fat 16%, chol 35 mg

Guacamole with Crudités

This reduced-fat version of guacamole combines avocado with cottage cheese, but tastes exceptionally rich. You can use nonfat cottage cheese to reduce the fat content even more. Use hard-skinned Hass variety avocados (black skin indicates ripeness), so the shells can be cut in half, scooped out, and stuffed. Believe it or not, an avocado pit placed into the center of a bowl of guacamole helps prevent the mixture from turning brown.

Guacamole

2	ripe avocados (preferably Hass), scooped out, with meat and shells reserved	2
2 tbl	fresh lemon juice	2 tbl
½ cup	low-fat cottage cheese	125 ml
3 tbl	fresh or bottled salsa	3 tbl
¼ cup	cooked shrimp meat	60 ml
3 cloves	garlic, minced	3 cloves
3 tbl	minced cilantro (coriander leaves)	3 tbl
1 head	curly endive or lettuce, separated into leaves	1 head
1 cup each	carrot sticks, cherry tomatoes, and raw cauliflower florets	250 ml each

1. In a blender or food processor, place avocado meat, lemon juice, cottage cheese, salsa, shrimp, garlic, and 1 tablespoon of the cilantro; purée. Spoon into scooped-out avocado shells.

2. Line a platter with endive and on it arrange stuffed shells surrounded by carrot sticks, cherry tomatoes, and cauliflower florets. Garnish with remaining cilantro. Serve slightly chilled or at room temperature.

Serves 12.
Each serving: cal 90, fat 5 g, cal from fat 26%, chol 10 mg

Salsa de Jalapeños Rojos

This tongue-tingling hot salsa is especially good with vegetables and fish. For information about roasting chiles, see page 77.

3	tomatoes	3
½	onion, chopped	½
½ tsp	salt	½ tsp
½ tbl	olive oil	½ tbl
4 cloves	garlic	4 cloves
4	fresh red jalapeño chiles, roasted, peeled, and cut into strips (see page 77)	4
2 tbl	chopped cilantro (coriander leaves)	2 tbl

1. Place tomatoes on a baking sheet and broil until fork-tender (about 10 minutes); peel. Place tomatoes, onion, and salt in a blender or food processor and blend briefly to an even consistency.

2. In a skillet heat oil. Add garlic, and toast to a golden brown. Remove garlic and discard. Add the chiles to the garlic-flavored oil and sauté briefly over high heat.

3. Add the tomato mixture and cilantro and cook over medium-high heat, stirring, until the sauce thickens (about 8–12 minutes). Serve warm.

Makes about 3 cups (700 ml), 6 servings.
Each serving: cal 42, fat 2 g, cal from fat 28%, chol 0 mg

SALSA DE CHIPOTLE

Smoke-dried jalapeño chiles (chipotles) add a wonderful smoky flavor to this hot table salsa. It is particularly good with pork, chicken, and fish dishes.

3	chipotle chiles	3
1 can (12 oz)	tomatillos, drained, or	1 can (350 g)
	9 fresh tomatillos, toasted	
2 cloves	garlic, chopped	2 cloves
3 tbl	minced white onion	3 tbl
¼ cup	coarsely chopped cilantro (coriander leaves)	60 ml

1. Toast the chiles on a comal or in a heavy skillet, turning until they are slightly crisp and lightly browned. Remove the stems and crumble the chiles into a blender. Grind the chiles until fine.

2. Add tomatillos, garlic, onion, and cilantro and blend briefly to a purée. Add ¼ cup (60 ml) of water in small amounts and blend to the desired consistency.

Makes about 1½ cups (350 ml), 4 servings.
Each serving: cal 49, fat 1 g, cal from fat 17%, chol 0 mg

"Little Whims"

In Mexico a unique system of snacking complements la comida, the mid-day meal. Street vendors, open-air markets, and restaurants offer an immense variety of mini-meals known as antojitos (literally "little whims" or "hankerings"). Designed for convenient consumption on the spot and often out of hand, these hors d'oeuvre-like snack foods include fresh fruit, fruit drinks, flavored ices, bakery goods, tacos, burritos, tamales, and skewered bits of meats, fish, or vegetables. There's something for any time of the day, and for every mood and taste. All in all, antojitos offer a light, healthy way to snack.

Corn Salsa

Enlivened with lime juice and fresh tomato, corn makes a piquant condiment for Enchiladas Del Rio (see recipe and photo on pages 66–67) or other dishes. You can double or triple the amount of jalapeño used in this recipe if you like plenty of heat in your salsa.

1 ear	corn or 1 cup (250 ml) frozen corn kernels	1 ear
1	plum tomato	1
2	green onions	2
1	jalapeño chile, minced	1
2 tbl	minced cilantro (coriander leaves)	2 tbl
2 tbl	lime juice (juice of 2 limes)	2 tbl
½ tsp	salt	½ tsp
⅛ tsp	freshly ground black pepper	⅛ tsp

1. If using fresh corn, slice kernels from ear and blanch for 1 minute. Drain and pat dry. If using frozen corn, defrost at room temperature before using.

2. Slice tomato in half, remove seeds, and cut into dice. Chop green onions into thin rings.

3. In a small mixing bowl, combine corn, tomato, green onions, chile, cilantro, lime juice, salt, and pepper. Chill, covered, before serving.

Makes about 1½ cups (350 ml), 4 servings.
Each serving: cal 51, fat .5 g, cal from fat 7%, chol 0 mg

Storing and Preserving Fresh Chiles

Stock up on fresh chiles whenever the supply is abundant, freeze or dry them, and you'll never be caught without this prime ingredient for Mexican cooking. Fresh mild chiles can be stored, loosely wrapped, in the refrigerator for 3–7 days; most fresh hot chile varieties will keep for up to 3 weeks.

To Freeze Fresh Chiles *For cooking chiles, follow the instructions for roasting chiles on page 77, then wrap chiles individually in plastic film. Place wrapped chiles in a plastic bag and seal tightly. For garnish or condiment chiles, first cook them for 1–2 minutes in a dry skillet over high heat or boil them 1–2 minutes in a small amount of water. Then freeze as for cooking chiles.*

To Dry Fresh Chiles *Green or red Anaheim chiles and yellow, green, or orange jalapeños are the best for drying.*

Indoors: Use a large needle and nylon thread. Push the needle through the stems, positioning chiles alternately to the left and right to allow air to circulate during drying. Hang strings of chiles (ristras) in an attic or other warm, dry place for about 3 weeks, until they shrivel and feel dry. If chiles start to mold, complete the drying process in an oven or dehydrator.

In an oven, dehydrator, or the sun: Dry whole, halved, or sliced chiles for 2–5 hours in a 140°F (60°C) oven or for 12–18 hours in a dehydrator set at 120°F (49°C). Whole chiles will dry in about 1–2 days in sunshine.

Dried chiles, packed in tightly sealed jars, will keep 3–4 months if stored in a cool, dry place, or longer if stored in the freezer. If condensation appears in jars (a sign that chiles are not fully dried), freeze or use chiles at once.

PICO DE GALLO

The name of this favorite Mexican antojito—"rooster's beak" in English—suggests the traditional manner in which this snack is consumed: held between fingers and thumb, in a way that suggests the pecking of a rooster. It makes a refreshing appetizer or simple first course.

1	jicama, peeled and cut into bite-sized wedges	1
3	oranges, peeled and cut into bite-sized wedges	3
to taste	salt	to taste
to taste	ground red chile, mild or hot	to taste

1. Arrange the jicama and orange wedges on a platter or individual plates.

2. Pass shakers of salt and ground chile, allowing each person to season to taste.

Serves 6.
Each serving: cal 34, fat .2 g, cal from fat 4%, chol 0 mg

Ensalada en Escabeche

This pickled vegetable salad is ready to eat in only a day.

2 lb	zucchini	900 g
1½ cups	sliced onion	350 ml
2 cups	carrot, cut into strips	500 ml
3 cups	celery, cut into strips	700 ml
12	radishes	12
¼ cup	salt	60 ml
3 cups	vinegar	700 ml
1½ cups	sugar	350 ml
1 tbl each	celery seed and fennel seed	1 tbl each
2 tbl	ground mustard seed	2 tbl
3	dried hot chiles, whole or coarsely chopped	3

In a bowl combine vegetables and salt. Cover with cold water and let stand 45 minutes. Drain. In a pan over low heat combine remaining ingredients. Bring to a simmer. Remove from heat and pour over vegetables. Let cool, then refrigerate at least 1 day. To serve, pour off liquid, reserving liquid. Arrange pickled vegetables on a plate. After serving return any leftover vegetables to liquid and store in refrigerator for up to 1 month.

Serves 12.
Each serving: cal 152, fat .7 g, cal from fat 4%, chol 0 mg

SEVICHE

For the best flavor, the fish should marinate at least 6 hours before you serve it.

1 lb	red snapper, cut into small cubes	450 g
1 cup	lime juice (juice of 10–12 limes)	250 ml
½	white onion, thinly sliced and separated into rings	½
1	tomato, peeled and diced	1
2	canned jalapeño chiles, seeded and chopped	2
½ tbl	olive oil	½ tbl
2 tbl	vinegar	2 tbl
2 tbl	chopped cilantro (coriander leaves)	2 tbl
as needed	green leaf lettuce	as needed
1	avocado, peeled and sliced (optional)	1
as needed	ground red chile, for garnish	as needed

1. Place the fish in a glass or porcelain bowl. Pour the lime juice over the fish, using enough juice to cover the fish, and marinate at least 4 hours or overnight in the refrigerator. Stir occasionally to be sure all surfaces of the fish are exposed to the juice.

2. Add the onion, tomato, chiles, oil, vinegar, and cilantro and mix gently. Refrigerate another 2 hours.

3. Just before serving place the lettuce leaves on individual plates, arrange the seviche on top, and garnish with the avocado slices, if used, and ground red chile.

Serves 4.
Each serving: cal 191, fat 4 g, cal from fat 19%, chol 42 mg

Preparing Seviche

Mexico, long on seacoasts and short on rivers and streams, enjoys a variety of fish and shellfish that is probably equaled only by that available in Asia. Few authentic Mexican fish and shellfish dishes are well known north of the border, but the marinated delicacy known as seviche is an exception.

Even if you don't like sushi, try seviche at least once! Refreshing and low in fat, this dish makes a fine hors d'oeuvre, appetizer, first course, or even a main-course salad (see recipe and photo on pages 24 and 25).

Made with raw fish marinated in fresh lime juice and other flavorful ingredients, seviche employs the simplest technique for food preservation—pickling, using an acid-based liquid, usually lime juice and/or vinegar. Firm, white-fleshed ocean fish such as tilefish, rockfish, or red snapper are good choices for seviche; salmon or shellfish (crab and shrimp) make delicious variations.

The cubed fish should remain in the marinade—refrigerated— until the flesh is opaque (at least 4 hours or overnight). The fish will develop a slightly pickled flavor and firm texture from the acids in the marinade. When the fish is ready to use, toss it with tomatoes, chiles, onions, and herbs; then cover and chill briefly before serving. Add a sprinkling of freshly ground black pepper, cayenne pepper, or ground red chile for color.

Sopa Taxco

Hot, crisply baked tortilla strips make this zesty soup from one of Mexico's mining regions especially hearty and satisfying (see photo on page 9).

1 tbl	olive oil	1 tbl
1	onion, thinly slivered	1
1 clove	garlic, minced	1 clove
½ tsp	ground cumin	½ tsp
2	canned green chiles, finely chopped	2
1 can (15 oz)	tomato sauce	1 can (430 g)
2 cups	defatted chicken stock	500 ml
4	corn tortillas, cut into thin strips	4
to taste	salt	to taste
¼ lb	cubed low-fat Monterey jack cheese (optional)	115 g
as needed	light sour cream, for garnish (optional)	as needed

1. In a large saucepan over medium heat, warm the oil and sauté onion, stirring until onion is soft. Mix in garlic and cumin; then add chiles, tomato sauce, stock, and 1 cup (250 ml) of water. Bring to a boil, cover, reduce heat, and simmer for 10 minutes.

2. While the soup simmers, heat oven to 325°F (160°C). Toast tortilla strips on a baking sheet in the oven until lightly browned (about 8–10 minutes). Place heatproof soup bowls on a baking sheet in oven during last 5 minutes.

3. Carefully remove hot soup bowls to a heatproof tray. Working quickly, divide hot tortilla strips among the bowls, salt lightly, and top with cheese cubes, if used. Ladle soup over all, and garnish with sour cream, if used. Serve at once.

Serves 4.
Each serving: cal 167, fat 5 g, cal from fat 27%, chol 1 mg

Sopa de Lima

Traditionally made with sour lemon, a fruit indigenous to the Yucatán, this soup is quite good when made with lime or lemon juice. Baked (not fried) tortilla chips make a light but satisfying accompaniment.

1 tbl	olive oil	1 tbl
½	onion, chopped	½
2	fresh jalapeño chiles	2
2	tomatoes, peeled and chopped	2
8 cups	defatted chicken stock	1.8 l
1	onion, quartered	1
3 cloves	garlic, coarsely chopped	3 cloves
6	peppercorns	6
½ tsp	dried thyme	½ tsp
1 tsp	salt	1 tsp
½ cup	lime juice (juice of 5–6 limes)	250 ml
2 cups	shredded chicken, light meat only	500 ml
⅓ cup	cilantro (coriander leaves)	85 ml
as needed	avocado slices and lime wedges, for garnish (optional)	as needed

1. In a large soup pot over medium heat, warm the oil and sauté the chopped onion and chiles until onion is soft. Add the tomatoes and cook until soft.

2. Add the stock to the soup pot with the quartered onion, garlic, peppercorns, thyme, and salt, and bring to a boil. Reduce heat and add the juice of 4 of the limes, plus a lime half. Simmer 30 minutes.

3. Remove the lime half, add the shredded chicken, and simmer 20 minutes. Stir in the cilantro.

4. Ladle soup into serving bowls. Garnish with avocado slices and lime wedges, if used.

Serves 8.
Each serving: cal 207, fat 6 g, cal from fat 24%, chol 35 mg

Sopa de Flor de Calabaza

The blossoms from pumpkin and squash plants (calabaza) were used in Aztec and Mayan cuisine and are still popular in traditional recipes such as this soup. Look for the fresh blossoms at farmers' markets during the peak of the summer harvest.

1 lb	squash or pumpkin blossoms	450 g
1 tsp	olive oil	1 tsp
½	onion, finely chopped	½
4 cups	defatted chicken stock	900 ml
1 sprig	epazote, if available (see below)	1 sprig
to taste	salt	to taste

1. Wash blossoms, pat dry with a paper towel, and coarsely chop.

2. In a soup pot over medium heat, warm the oil and gently sauté the blossoms and onion. Add stock and epazote. Simmer 20 minutes.

3. Remove the epazote, add salt to taste, and serve.

Serves 6.
Each serving: cal 71, fat 3 g, cal from fat 32%, chol 2 mg

Epazote

With a distinctive flavor and aftertaste and an unusual odor that takes getting used to, epazote is a classic accompaniment to Mexican dishes like the one above, as well as rice, black beans, corn, mushrooms, and fish. Indigenous to central Mexico, epazote is also known as wormseed (Chenopodium ambrosioides) and is related botanically to spinach and lamb's quarters. It is available fresh or dried in some supermarkets and most Latino markets. Reputedly easier to grow than to describe, epazote seed is available through a number of garden seed catalogs.

GAZPACHO CORTÉS

A traditional chilled vegetable soup popular in both Spain and Mexico, gazpacho is sometimes blended to a purée, sometimes left chunky. Gazpacho is usually tomato-based, but here the soup base is made with fresh green vegetables and a defatted chicken stock flavored with snow peas (see photo on page 10). For a sweeter taste purée or chop the cooked snow peas and add them to the soup stock.

6 cups	snow peas	1.4 l
3 cups	defatted chicken stock	700 ml
1	onion, finely minced	1
2 cloves	garlic, pressed	2 cloves
½ cup	chopped green bell pepper	125 ml
1	jalapeño chile, seeded and finely chopped	1
¾ cup	chopped celery stalk and leaves	175 ml
2 tsp	lemon juice	2 tsp
1 tsp	lime juice	1 tsp
½ tsp	dried tarragon	½ tsp
½ tsp	ground cumin	½ tsp
to taste	cayenne pepper	to taste
to taste	salt	to taste
as needed	chopped fresh tomatillos, for garnish (optional)	as needed

1. In a stockpot place snow peas and stock; bring to a boil. Lower heat and simmer 35 minutes. Strain out snow peas and reserve for another use or discard.

2. Add onion, garlic, bell pepper, chile, celery, lemon juice, lime juice, tarragon, and cumin; chill. Add cayenne and salt, to taste, and serve cold, garnished with chopped tomatillos, if used.

Serves 6.
Each serving: cal 101, fat 1 g, cal from fat 11%, chol 0 mg

Sopa de Melón

Perfect for summer, this cool and creamy melon soup is delicate in color and flavor. It can be served for any light meal, from brunch to dinner.

½ cup	half-and-half	125 ml
1 cup	skim milk	250 ml
1 cup	cooked, peeled, diced potato	250 ml
3 cups	peeled, diced cantaloupe	700 ml
¼ cup	dry sherry	60 ml
pinch	salt	pinch
to taste	freshly ground nutmeg, for garnish	to taste

1. Place half-and-half, skim milk, potato, and cantaloupe in a blender or food processor. Blend to a smooth purée. Stir in sherry. Add salt.

2. Serve chilled, sprinkled with freshly ground nutmeg.

Serves 6.
Each serving: cal 90, fat 3 g, cal from fat 28%, chol 8 mg

Sopa de Pollo

This Mexican version of chicken soup contains chayote, a pale green squash native to Mexico that is available in most Latino markets.

1	onion, chopped	1
2 cloves	garlic, minced	2 cloves
1 tbl	olive oil	1 tbl
3½ lb	chicken, cut up, skin removed	1.6 kg
1 tsp	salt	1 tsp
2	chayotes, halved lengthwise	2
6	carrots, halved lengthwise, then cut into thirds	6
3 ears	corn, cut into thirds	3 ears
3	zucchini, cut into chunks	3
as needed	lime wedges, oregano, and fresh or bottled salsa, for garnish	as needed

1. In a soup pot over medium heat, sauté onion and garlic in oil. Add chicken, salt, and cover with water. Bring almost to a boil, reduce heat, cover, and simmer until chicken is tender (about 30–40 minutes).

2. In another pot, cover chayotes with water and bring to a boil. Reduce heat, cover, and cook until almost tender (about 15 minutes). Drain chayotes and allow to cool. Peel and cut into large chunks.

3. Remove chicken from soup pot; debone, and cut the meat into serving-sized pieces. Skim any fat from cooking liquid and return liquid to soup pot.

4. Add carrots and corn to soup pot and simmer 10 minutes. Add zucchini and cook an additional 10 minutes. Add chayote and chicken pieces and continue cooking until zucchini is tender and soup is heated.

5. Divide chicken and vegetables among soup bowls; ladle cooking liquid over all. Serve garnishes in separate bowls.

Serves 6.
Each serving: cal 421, fat 11 g, cal from fat 24%, chol 183 mg

Ensalada de Frijoles

This unusual and delicious salad deserves a fresh salsa like Salsa de Jalapeños Rojos (see page 17), although you can use bottled salsa if you're pressed for time. Cook the beans the day before making the salad and chill them overnight. This salad will keep for three days in a covered container in the refrigerator (see photo on page 10).

4 cups	cooked lima beans	900 ml
1 cup	cooked pinto beans (see page 74)	250 ml
2 cups	fresh or bottled salsa	500 ml
2 cups	chopped green leaf lettuce	500 ml
2	tomatoes, chopped	2
3 tbl	chopped cilantro (coriander leaves)	3 tbl

1. Toss lima and pinto beans with salsa and marinate for 4 hours.

2. Place lettuce and tomatoes in a salad bowl and spoon on beans; top with cilantro. Serve chilled.

Serves 6.
Each serving: cal 233, fat 4 g, cal from fat 15%, chol 1 mg

ENSALADA DE NOCHE BUENA

In Mexico this colorful fruit and vegetable salad is traditionally served on Christmas Eve (Noche Buena).

1	jicama, peeled and cut into bite-sized pieces	1
2	oranges, peeled, sliced, and quartered	2
3 slices	fresh pineapple, peeled and cut into bite-sized pieces	3 slices
2	bananas, sliced	2
1 can (8 oz)	diced beets	1 can (225 g)
½ head	iceberg lettuce, shredded	½ head
½ cup	unsalted peanuts	125 ml
1	pomegranate, seeds removed and reserved	1

1. In a large bowl mix together the jicama, oranges, and pineapple and chill for at least 1 hour.

2. Just before serving add bananas and beets.

3. Line a salad bowl or platter with lettuce and arrange fruit on the lettuce. Garnish with peanuts and pomegranate seeds.

Serves 8.
Each serving: cal 406, fat 7 g, cal from fat 14%, chol 0 mg

JICAMA

With a sweet flavor and satisfyingly crunchy texture similar to water chestnuts or radishes, this native Mexican root vegetable makes a nice addition to crudité platters, salads, and vegetable dishes. Its light brown skin and white flesh offer visual appeal, and it stays crisp even when cooked. Jicama has been used in many Asian dishes since the Spanish first exported it to the Philippines during the 17th century, so if no supermarkets or Latino markets in your area stock jicama, look for it at Asian markets.

Ensalada de Jicama

Jicama, orange, and cucumber tossed in a light dressing create a tangy-sweet salad with just enough crunch to be interesting.

Oil and Vinegar Dressing

2 cloves	garlic, crushed	2 cloves
1 tbl	white wine vinegar	1 tbl
½ tsp	salt	½ tsp
¼ tsp	freshly ground black pepper	¼ tsp
1 tsp	prepared Dijon mustard	1 tsp
2 tbl	olive oil	2 tbl
1	jicama, peeled and diced	1
1	cucumber, scored with a fork and thinly sliced	1
3	oranges, peeled, sliced, and quartered	3
6 leaves	green leaf lettuce	6 leaves

1. Combine garlic, vinegar, salt, and pepper in a lidded jar. Shake until salt dissolves. Add 1 teaspoon cold water, mustard, and oil; shake until thoroughly blended. Set aside.

2. In a bowl mix together jicama, cucumber, and oranges. Toss with dressing and chill until ready to serve.

3. Just before serving, line a platter or 6 individual plates with lettuce leaves and arrange salad on the lettuce.

Serves 6.
Each serving: cal 64, fat 3 g, cal from fat 28%, chol 0 mg

Ensalada de Nopalitos

Red onions, tomatoes, ripe olives, cilantro, and a flavorful dressing make a stunning cactus salad with a special flavor. Your adventuresome friends will love the idea of eating nopales (prickly pear cactus). Canned nopales are available in Latino markets and gourmet food shops, but if you're fortunate enough to have a prickly pear cactus available for harvesting, here's how to prepare fresh nopales for cooking:

Select young, firm cactus pads, trim off the spines, and dice the cactus flesh. Place in boiling, salted water to cover; reduce heat and simmer until tender (about 10–15 minutes). Rinse and drain several times until the cactus no longer feels slippery. The nopales are then ready to use.

3 cups	freshly prepared nopales, or	700 ml
	1 jar (16 oz or 450 g) nopales, rinsed and drained	
1	red onion, thinly sliced and separated into rings	1
3	tomatoes, chopped	3
2 tbl	chopped cilantro (coriander leaves)	2 tbl
1 recipe	Oil and Vinegar Dressing (see page 38)	1 recipe
1 can (4¼ oz)	sliced ripe olives,	1 can (120 g)
	drained, for garnish (optional)	

Mix together nopales, onion, tomatoes, and cilantro. Toss with dressing, garnish with olives, if used, and serve.

Serves 6.
Each serving: cal 67, fat 3 g, cal from fat 33%, chol 0 mg

Ejotes y Papas

The delicious combination of fresh green beans and potatoes (ejotes y papas) with a light dressing makes a perfect lunch salad.

2 recipes	Oil and Vinegar Dressing (see page 38)	2 recipes
6	red potatoes, quartered	6
1 lb	green beans, ends removed	450 g
2 tbl	chopped cilantro (coriander leaves)	2 tbl
1 tbl	capers	1 tbl
6 leaves	green leaf lettuce	6 leaves

1. Prepare dressing and set aside.

2. Place potatoes in a steamer and arrange green beans on top. Cover tightly and steam until barely tender (about 15 minutes). Do not overcook. Place vegetables in a bowl and pour in the dressing. Toss to coat, then chill, covered, for 3 hours.

3. Just before serving mix in the cilantro and capers. Line a platter or individual plates with lettuce leaves and arrange vegetables on the lettuce.

Serves 6.
Each serving: cal 161, fat 5 g, cal from fat 26%, chol 0 mg

Main Dishes and Accompaniments

Succulent Enchiladas Verdes de Mariscos (see page 45), hearty Turkey Chili Burritos (see page 57), or colorful Pollo en Salsa (see page 52) served with classic Mexican side dishes, Arroz Yucatán (see page 70) and Frijoles (see page 74) . . . Dishes like these can cinch your reputation as a master of low-fat Mexican cuisine.

Enchiladas Verdes de Mariscos

These flavorful seafood enchiladas are mildly spicy .

2 tbl	olive oil	2 tbl
2 tbl	minced garlic	2 tbl
3	green onions, minced	3
1	fresh or canned green (Anaheim) chile, finely chopped	1
1 can (12 oz)	tomatillos, puréed	1 can (350 g)
to taste	salt	to taste
¼ cup	chopped cilantro (coriander leaves)	60 ml
2 cups	cooked shellfish (shrimp, crabmeat, scallops, or a combination)	500 ml
8	corn tortillas	8
½ cup	light sour cream (optional)	125 ml
½ cup	grated low-fat Monterey jack cheese (optional)	125 ml

1. Preheat oven to 400°F (205°C). In a large skillet over moderate heat, warm oil and add garlic, green onions, and chile, cooking until vegetables are soft. Stir in the tomatillo purée, reduce heat, and cook 10 minutes more, adding water if mixture seems too dry. Add salt.

2. In a bowl combine cilantro and shellfish; stir in a small amount of the sauce. Moisten bottom of a shallow 8- by 13-inch (20- by 32.5-cm) baking dish with about ¼ cup (60 ml) of the sauce.

3. Dip a tortilla into the simmering sauce until soft and pliable (about 30 seconds); transfer to baking dish. Place ¼ cup (60 ml) of the seafood across the center of tortilla and roll it into a cylinder. Repeat with remaining tortillas, fitting them snugly side by side. Pour remaining sauce over enchiladas and top with sour cream and cheese, if used. Bake 10 minutes and serve.

Makes 8 enchiladas, 8 servings.
Each serving: cal 184, fat 5 g, cal from fat 25%, chol 115 mg

Camarones con Ajo

These garlic-dipped shrimp are grilled to perfection over hot coals. Serve with Fideo (see recipe on page 68 and photo on page 47), warm tortillas, and a tossed green salad.

1½ lb	medium to large shrimp	680 g
1 tbl	butter or oil	1 tbl
3 cloves	garlic, pressed	3 cloves
pinch	mild ground chile	pinch
1 tbl	lime juice (juice of 1 lime)	1 tbl

1. Peel shrimp, leaving the tail for a handle. Remove vein.

2. In a small pan melt the butter. Add garlic, ground chile, and lime juice. Simmer 1 minute.

3. Dip each shrimp in garlic butter and place on skewers (the double-prong type of skewer will keep the shrimp flat). Grill over hot coals, basting with the remaining garlic butter, turning once and cooking only until pink (about 3 minutes). Take care not to overcook the shrimp or they will become tough. Serve at once.

Serves 4.
Each serving: cal 210, fat 6 g, cal from fat 26%, chol 266 mg

PESCADO BORRACHO

The name "drunken fish" (pescado borracho) suggests the way in which this fish is cooked—poached in wine. The fresh fillets are spiked with sprigs of cilantro and chopped chiles, then poached in wine for a wonderfully light main course dish.

8	sole fillets	8
1 tsp	salt	1 tsp
1/2 tsp	freshly ground black pepper	1/2 tsp
24 sprigs	cilantro (coriander leaves)	24 sprigs
2	jalapeño or serrano chiles, seeded, deveined, and minced	2
2 cups	dry white wine	500 ml
2 tbl	lime juice (juice of 2 limes)	2 tbl
8	thin slices of lime	8
1/2 cup	pomegranate seeds	125 ml

1. Pat fillets dry. Place outer side of fillet down and sprinkle with salt and pepper. Place 2 sprigs of the cilantro and some of the chopped chiles in the center of each fillet. Fold the fillets in thirds and place folded side down in a wide, shallow saucepan.

2. Pour wine and 4 cups (900 ml) of water over fish. The fish should be completely immersed. Cover and bring to a simmer. Poach 8–10 minutes. Remove from heat and cool in poaching liquid. When cool, remove from liquid.

3. To serve, sprinkle fish with the remaining cilantro and lime juice. Top each fillet with a slice of lime and some pomegranate seeds.

Serves 8.
Each serving: cal 149, fat .9 g, cal from fat 6%, chol 0 mg

Pescado en Salsa Verde

For an easy, elegant, low-fat dinner, serve these salsa-spiced fish-and-vegetables packets (see photo on page 10).

1½ lb	fresh salmon, cod, or red snapper, cut into 1-inch- (2.5-cm-) thick fillets	680 g
1 tsp	olive oil	1 tsp
¼ cup	dry white wine	60 ml
1 cup	chopped onion	250 ml
⅓ cup	chopped green bell pepper	85 ml
1 clove	garlic, minced	1 clove
1 cup	chopped fresh tomatillos	250 ml
1 tsp	ground cumin	1 tsp
2 tbl	chopped chiles en escabeche (pickled hot chiles)	2 tbl
1 tsp each	lemon juice and lime juice	1 tsp each
⅓ cup	chopped cilantro (coriander leaves)	85 ml

1. Preheat oven to 475°F (240°C). Cut fish fillets into 4 servings. Carefully remove bones. Place each portion on top of a sheet of parchment paper, cut 3 or 4 times larger than each fillet.

2. In a skillet heat oil and wine; add onion and sauté until soft. Add bell pepper, garlic, tomatillos, and cumin. Continue cooking for 8 minutes. Add remaining ingredients and cook 3 more minutes.

3. Spoon sautéed vegetables over portions of fish. Fold parchment like an envelope, sealing fish completely. Place on a baking sheet. Bake parchment packets for 10 minutes. Serve by cutting packets down the center and placing on a platter or individual plates.

Serves 4.
Each serving: cal 252, fat 8 g, cal from fat 29%, chol 89 mg

MEXICAN-STYLE MARINADES FOR FISH

Spoon either of these simple, low-fat marinades over fish about 15 minutes before cooking. Use any remaining marinade to baste fish as it poaches, bakes, or grills:

- *Slice a small onion into rings and combine with 2 cloves pressed garlic and juice of 2 limes (see photo above).*

- *Combine juice of 1 lemon with a tablespoon of chopped cilantro and a sprinkling of crushed dried hot chile or cayenne pepper.*

Pollo en Salsa

This recipe is great for a picnic lunch, served with Gazpacho Cortés (see page 31), perhaps a crisp salad, and Plato de Frutas (see page 90) for dessert. Use bottled salsa or Salsa de Chipotle (see page 18)—whichever suits your taste and tolerance for heat and spiciness.

4	half-breasts of chicken, skin removed	4
1 cup	fresh or bottled salsa	250 ml
1 tbl	rice vinegar	1 tbl
1 tbl	minced cilantro (coriander leaves)	1 tbl
as needed	lemon slices or yellow chiles, for garnish	as needed

1. Preheat oven to 375°F (190°C). Place chicken breasts in a medium-sized baking dish.

2. Mix salsa, vinegar, and cilantro. Spoon over chicken.

3. Bake chicken for 20–25 minutes, uncovered. Serve hot or cold, garnished with lemon slices.

Serves 4.
Each serving: cal 152, fat 4 g, cal from fat 24%, chol 65 mg

Pollo Almendrado

From the tropical regions of Mexico comes this fragrant chicken dish baked in a sauce of pineapple, grapes, herbs, and spices. Serve with Arroz Yucatán (see page 70) and a salad.

¼ cup	whole almonds, blanched	60 m
1½ tbl	olive oil	1½ tbl
6	chicken breast halves, skin removed	6
½ cup	crushed pineapple	125 ml
1 cup	fresh, seedless grapes or 1 can (8 oz or 225 g) whole grapes, drained	250 ml
1 cup	orange juice	250 ml
1 cup	dry white wine	250 ml
2 tbl	honey	2 tbl
⅛ tsp	ground cinnamon	⅛ tsp
⅛ tsp	ground cloves	⅛ tsp
⅛ tsp	dried thyme	⅛ tsp
as needed	slivers of orange zest, for garnish	as needed

1. Toast almonds in a 300°F (150°C) oven for 30 minutes. Cool and grind two-thirds of the almonds in a blender until fine. Coarsely chop the remaining almonds and combine with ground almonds.

2. In a skillet over medium heat warm the oil and sauté the chicken pieces for 10 minutes on each side. Place browned chicken pieces in a single layer in a shallow glass baking pan.

3. Preheat oven to 325°F (160°C). In a medium bowl combine pineapple, grapes, orange juice, wine, honey, cinnamon, cloves, thyme, and almonds, and pour over the chicken. Bake for 40 minutes, basting several times. Increase oven to 350°F (175°C) and bake 10 minutes longer. Garnish with orange zest and serve.

Serves 6.
Each serving: cal 255, fat 5 g, cal from fat 19%, chol 65 mg

PASTEL VERDURAS

A cornmeal crust envelopes this hearty vegetable pie (pastel verduras).

2 cups	finely ground yellow cornmeal	500 ml
½ cup	pastry flour	125 ml
2 tsp	baking powder	2 tsp
½ tsp	salt	½ tsp
2½ tsp	olive oil	2½ tsp
1	onion, chopped	1
3 cloves	garlic, minced	3 cloves
1 cup	chopped red bell pepper	250 ml
½ cup	diced carrot	125 ml
3 cups	cooked kidney beans	700 ml
1 cup	thick tomato sauce	250 ml
2 tsp	chili powder	2 tsp
1 tsp	ground cumin	1 tsp
2 tbl	dry white wine	2 tbl

1. Preheat oven to 350°F (175°C). In a medium bowl blend cornmeal, flour, baking powder, and salt. Stir in 1 cup (250 ml) water and knead until smooth. Lightly coat a 9- by 12-inch (22.5- by 30-cm) baking dish with ½ teaspoon of the oil; pat half the dough into bottom of dish. On waxed paper, spread remaining dough into a rectangle the size of the baking dish. Set aside.

2. In a skillet over medium heat, warm remaining oil; sauté onion until soft. Add garlic, bell pepper, and carrot and cook 5 minutes, stirring frequently. Add remaining ingredients, cover, and simmer until vegetables are tender. Spoon vegetable filling over crust in baking dish and top with reserved crust. Bake until brown and bubbly (about 40 minutes). Serve hot.

Serves 8.
Each serving: cal 276, fat 3 g, cal from fat 8%, chol 0 mg

Turkey Chili Burritos

Homemade chunky-style turkey chili wrapped in warm flour tortillas makes a fast, nutritious meal that's low in fat.

1 cup	minced onion	250 ml
1 tsp	olive oil	1 tsp
½ cup	defatted chicken stock	125 ml
1 tbl	minced garlic	1 tbl
4 cups	skinned and diced turkey, light meat only	900 ml
½ cup	diced celery	125 ml
½ cup	chopped carrot	125 ml
¼ cup	minced parsley	60 ml
1 cup	diced tomatoes	250 ml
½ tsp	ground cloves	½ tsp
to taste	chili powder	to taste
½ tsp	hot-pepper sauce	½ tsp
1 can (4 oz)	green chiles, chopped	1 can (115 g)
to taste	salt and freshly ground black pepper	to taste
12	flour tortillas	12
½ cup	grated low-fat Cheddar cheese	125 ml

1. In a Dutch oven over medium-high heat, sauté onion in oil and stock until soft. Add garlic, turkey, celery, carrot, parsley, and tomatoes and sauté, stirring frequently, for 10 minutes.

2. Add 1 cup (250 ml) of water, cloves, chili powder, hot-pepper sauce, and green chiles. Lower heat, cover, and cook for 25 minutes. Add salt and pepper to taste.

3. Warm tortillas by wrapping in foil and placing in oven for 5 minutes at 200°F (95°C).

4. To serve, spoon about ⅓ cup (85 ml) chili onto each tortilla, sprinkle with grated cheese, and fold tortilla to encase filling. Repeat with remaining tortillas and filling.

Makes 12 burritos, 6 servings.
Each serving: cal 482, fat 10 g, cal from fat 19%, chol 93 mg

CHIHUAHUA CHILAQUILES

This Mexican turkey stew works equally well with chicken or even lean beef, as shown in the photo on page 59.

2	onions, diced	2
4 cloves	garlic, sliced	4 cloves
2 tbl	olive oil	2 tbl
6	dried Anaheim chiles, chopped	6
2–3	jalapeño chiles, sliced	2–3
7 cups	defatted chicken stock	1.6 l
6 cups	cooked shredded turkey, light meat only	1.4 l
10 oz	frozen corn kernels	285 g
1 can (15 oz)	plum tomatoes, drained and diced	1 can (430 g)
1 tbl each	toasted cumin seed and salt	1 tbl each
¼ tsp	freshly ground black pepper	¼ tsp
½ tsp	hot-pepper flakes	½ tsp
6	corn tortillas, cut into thin strips	6
1 cup	light sour cream, for garnish (optional)	250 ml
¼ cup	sliced green onions, for garnish	60 ml
6 sprigs	cilantro (coriander leaves), for garnish	6 sprigs

1. In a large saucepan over medium heat, sauté onion and garlic in oil until softened and translucent (4–5 minutes). Add chiles, stock, turkey, corn, tomatoes, cumin, salt, black pepper, and hot-pepper flakes. Reduce heat and simmer, uncovered, for 45 minutes.

2. While chilaquiles simmer, heat oven to 350°F (175°C). Toast tortilla strips on a baking sheet in the oven until lightly browned (8–10 minutes); watch to see that they do not burn. Remove from oven and set aside.

3. Serve chilaquiles in shallow soup bowls, topped with toasted tortilla strips, sour cream, if used, green onions, and cilantro sprigs.

Serves 6.
Each serving: cal 547, fat 12 g, cal from fat 19%, chol 136 mg

ENSALADA DE CARNE

If you like taco salad, you'll love this version made with marinated cooked brisket. You can also use lean roast beef, chicken, or turkey. Cebolla en Lima—pickled onions—are a classic accompaniment, and they're fat-free. The tortilla chips should be baked, not fried. Traditionally garnished with queso fresco—a fresh, unripened cheese popular in Mexico—this salad can be crowned with crumbled feta cheese, which is relatively low in fat and a good substitute for the Mexican cheese.

Cebolla en Lima

¼ cup	lime juice (juice of 3 limes)	60 ml
1	red onion, thinly sliced and separated into rings	1
1 tbl	cilantro (coriander leaves), lightly packed	1 tbl
2 recipes	Oil and Vinegar Dressing (see page 38)	2 recipes
⅓ cup	fresh or bottled salsa	85 ml
3 cups	cooked lean beef brisket, julienned	700 ml
1 head	green leaf lettuce, torn into pieces	1 head
4	tomatoes, cut into wedges	4
2 cups	shredded red cabbage	500 ml
¼ cup	sliced black olives (optional)	60 ml
¼ cup	garbanzo beans, cooked and drained	60 ml
32	baked tortilla chips	32
as needed	crumbled feta cheese (optional)	as needed

1. To prepare Cebolla en Lima, juice limes into a glass bowl; add onion rings and cilantro. Cover and marinate, refrigerated, for 3–6 hours before using. (Onions will keep for 2–3 weeks in the refrigerator.)

2. In a small bowl combine dressing and salsa. Place beef in a medium bowl and pour marinade over it; marinate, covered, in refrigerator for 2–3 hours.

3. In a large bowl combine lettuce, tomatoes, cabbage, olives (if used), and garbanzo beans. Add the meat mixture and lightly toss.

4. Divide salad among 8 chilled plates. Arrange tortilla chips alongside and garnish salad with marinated onions and feta cheese, if used.

Serves 8.
Each serving: cal 263, fat 9 g, cal from fat 31%, chol 53 mg

FAJITAS LAREDO

Fajitas are a flavorful combination of beef (as shown on page 63) or, in this version, chicken strips sautéed with onions, mushrooms, and fiery chiles. The mixture is rolled into warm flour tortillas at the table.

1 cup	sliced onions	250 ml
1 cup	sliced mushrooms	250 ml
1 tsp	olive oil	1 tsp
⅓ cup	dry sherry	85 ml
1 lb	skinless, boneless chicken breast	450 g
2	serrano or jalapeño chiles, seeded and minced	2
½ tsp	cumin seed	½ tsp
¼ tsp	ground coriander	¼ tsp
1 tsp	minced cilantro (coriander leaves)	1 tsp
6	flour tortillas	6
½ cup	fresh or bottled salsa	125 ml
½	avocado, thinly sliced	½
1 cup	nonfat yogurt	250 ml

1. In a large skillet over medium-high heat, sauté onions and mushrooms in oil and sherry for 10 minutes. Cut chicken into 1½-inch (3.75-cm) strips and add to sauté, cooking for 2 minutes more. Add chiles, cumin, coriander, and cilantro, and cook 3 more minutes, stirring frequently.

2. Warm tortillas by wrapping in foil and placing in oven for 5 minutes at 200°F (95°C). Set out bowls of salsa, sliced avocado, and yogurt. Wrap warmed tortillas in clean cloth napkin. Serve fajita filling directly from skillet or in prewarmed dish and assemble fajitas at the table.

Makes 6 fajitas, 6 servings.
Each serving: cal 260, fat 7 g, cal from fat 27%, chol 45 mg

ADOBO

The spicy chile purée that gives this dish its name does double duty as marinade and basting sauce for the pork. Reserve this luxurious barbecue for very special occasions.

5	dried ancho chiles	5
3	dried California chiles	3
4 cloves	garlic, minced	4 cloves
1 tsp	dried oregano	1 tsp
½ tsp	ground cumin	½ tsp
¼ tsp	ground cloves	¼ tsp
1 tbl	salt	1 tbl
½ cup	wine vinegar	125 ml
3 lb	lean pork tenderloin	1.4 kg
10	flour tortillas, wrapped in foil and warmed on the grill	10
as needed	fresh or bottled salsa, for garnish	as needed

1. Remove the stems and seeds from the chiles and discard. Place chiles in a saucepan and add water just to cover. Bring to a boil, reduce heat, and simmer for 5 minutes. Set aside to steep for 30 minutes. Drain the chiles.

2. Place chiles and remaining ingredients except meat, tortillas, and salsa into a blender or food processor and purée. Slice the tenderloin into 10 portions. Spread the chile purée over the meat, covering all sides of each portion. Reserve any remaining chile purée. Rub purée in well and roast immediately, or, for maximum flavor, cover with waxed paper and allow to season in the refrigerator for 1–3 days.

3. Prepare a hot charcoal or mesquite fire for grilling. Grill pork, basting occasionally with any remaining chile purée, until well done or to individual preference. Serve with salsa and warm tortillas.

Serves 10.
Each serving: cal 504, fat 17 g, cal from fat 30%, chol 110 mg

ENCHILADAS DEL RIO

These border-style vegetarian enchiladas can be prepared ahead and heated in the oven just before serving time.

1	bell pepper	1
1	jalapeño chile	1
2 cans (28 oz each)	plum tomatoes	2 cans (800 g each)
2 tbl	olive oil	2 tbl
2	onions, minced	2
6 cloves	garlic, minced	6 cloves
1½ tsp	ground cumin	1½ tsp
2½ tsp	salt	2½ tsp
12	flour tortillas	12
½ recipe	Frijoles (see page 74)	½ recipe
8 oz	grated low-fat Monterey jack or Colby cheese	225 g
½ recipe	Guacamole (see page 16), for garnish	½ recipe
1 recipe	Corn Salsa (see page 20)	1 recipe

1. To prepare sauce, remove and discard seeds from bell pepper and jalapeño; dice peppers finely. Purée tomatoes in a blender. In a large saucepan over medium heat, warm the oil and sauté onion and garlic for 5 minutes. Add the peppers, tomato purée, cumin, and salt. Bring to a boil, reduce heat, and simmer for 30 minutes. Cool slightly.

2. Preheat oven to 350°F (175°C). Wrap tortillas in foil and warm in oven for 8–10 minutes. Warm the frijoles in a saucepan. Pour 2 cups (500 ml) of the sauce into a 10- by 15-inch (25- by 37.5-cm) baking dish.

3. Remove tortillas from oven and remove one from foil. Spoon about ¼ cup (125 ml) frijoles onto a tortilla and sprinkle with about 2 tablespoons cheese. Drizzle with 1 tablespoon of the sauce. Roll tortilla around filling, leaving ends open, to form enchilada and place in baking dish. Repeat with remaining tortillas.

4. Pour remaining sauce over enchiladas and sprinkle with remaining cheese. Bake until cheese is melted and filling is heated (about 25–30 minutes). Spoon dollops of Guacamole over enchiladas for garnish and serve with Corn Salsa.

Makes 12 enchiladas, 6 servings.
Each serving: cal 866, fat 23 g, cal from fat 23%, chol 18 mg

FIDEO

Although not commonly served in restaurants, this dish is a favorite in Mexican homes (see photo on page 47). Remember that vermicelli scorches easily and needs careful attention during sautéing.

1 pkg (8 oz)	coiled vermicelli	1 pkg (225 g)
2 tbl	olive oil	2 tbl
1	onion, chopped	1
1 clove	garlic, minced	1 clove
1	Anaheim chile, seeded and chopped (optional)	1
1	tomato, chopped	1
2½ cups	defatted chicken stock	600 ml
to taste	salt	to taste
as needed	light sour cream and fresh cilantro (coriander leaves), for garnish (optional)	as needed

1. To crumble the vermicelli, roll a rolling pin over the un-opened package. In a large skillet over medium heat, warm the oil and sauté the vermicelli until golden, stirring constantly.

2. Push the vermicelli to one side, add onion, garlic, and chile, if used, and cook until the onion is soft. Add tomato and stir to mix vermicelli with chile-tomato mixture.

3. Add stock and bring to a boil. Reduce heat, cover, and simmer until the liquid has been absorbed (15–20 minutes). Add salt.

4. Serve garnished with a dollop of sour cream and cilantro, if used.

Serves 6.
Each serving: cal 217, fat 6 g, cal from fat 24%, chol 1 mg

MAKING A SOPA SECA

Unlike sopas aguadas ("wet soups"), sopas secas ("dry soups") consist of rice or pasta cooked in flavored liquid. The following instructions are for Fideo (see recipe on opposite page), made with vermicelli. Other sopas are made with alphabet noodles or rice.

2. Push the browned vermicelli to one side of the pan and add vegetables, cooking just until tender.

1. Take a rolling pin and roll over the unopened package of vermicelli until it is crumbled. In a large skillet heat oil. Add the crumbled vermicelli, stir constantly (to avoid scorching) until golden brown.

3. After the vegetables have cooked, mix them with the vermicelli. Add boiling stock, cover, and steam until liquid is absorbed (about 15–20 minutes).

Arroz Yucatán

This rice, colored and delicately flavored with achiote (annatto seed), is typical of the Yucatán. Achiote, the small, brick-red seed of the annatto tree, imparts a bright yellow color to the rice and gives it a flavor that is especially tasty with fish dishes. Look for achiote in Latino, Caribbean, and Philippine markets.

3 tsp	achiote (annatto seed)	3 tsp
1 tbl	olive oil	1 tbl
2 cups	long-grain rice, washed and drained	500 ml
1	onion, chopped	1
2 cloves	garlic, minced	2 cloves
4 cups	defatted chicken stock or water	900 ml
2 tsp	salt	2 tsp

1. In a medium saucepan over low heat, sauté the achiote in oil. Remove the seeds from the oil when they are dark brown, and discard seeds. The oil will be dark orange in color.

2. Add the rice to the oil and sauté for about 5 minutes. Add the onion and garlic and cook until onion is soft.

3. In a separate pan bring stock to a boil. Add boiling stock to rice along with salt. Bring mixture to a boil, reduce heat, cover, and cook until liquid is absorbed (20–25 minutes).

Serves 6.
Each serving: cal 216, fat 3 g, cal from fat 14%, chol 0 mg

FRIJOLES NEGROS

Black beans (also called turtle beans) are frequently a part of the cuisine in the southern regions of Mexico. They are cooked with a sprig of fresh epazote, a Mexican herb that adds a subtle flavor to the beans and is traditionally believed to reduce flatulence (see page 30). There is no substitute for epazote, but if you can't find it at the farmers' market or in a Latino market, the beans will be delicious without it.

2 cups	black beans	500 ml
2 tbl	olive oil	2 tbl
2 tsp	salt	2 tsp
2 sprigs	fresh epazote, if available	2 sprigs
as needed	light sour cream, minced onion, and jalapeño slices, for garnish (optional)	as needed

1. Pick through and wash the beans but do not soak them.

2. In a large pot place beans, 8 cups (1.8 l) of water, and oil. Bring to a boil, reduce heat, cover, and simmer until the skins have begun to split (about 2 hours). Add salt and epazote, if used, and continue to cook for another hour, or until very tender.

3. Serve beans, along with some of their cooking liquid, in small bowls. Add garnishes, if used.

Serves 6.
Each serving: cal 261, fat 6 g, cal from fat 19%, chol 0 mg

FRIJOLES

In traditional Mexican cooking beans are rarely soaked overnight before cooking. In this contemporary recipe, the beans are first soaked to reduce cooking time and then slow-cooked for optimum flavor. For an even faster method, quick-soak the beans: cover them with water and boil for 2 minutes, skimming off any froth that appears. Turn off the heat and let the beans stand for an hour, then cook them until tender.

1 lb	pinto beans, soaked overnight in water to cover, drained	450 g
1	onion, coarsely chopped	1
2 cloves	garlic, minced	2 cloves
¼ tsp	hot-pepper flakes	¼ tsp
1	onion, finely chopped	1
2 tbl	olive oil	2 tbl
1	tomato, peeled, seeded, and coarsely chopped	1
to taste	salt and freshly ground black pepper	to taste

1. In a large pot place beans, 8 cups (1.8 l) water, the coarsely chopped onion, garlic, and hot-pepper flakes. Bring to a boil, skimming any froth that appears. Lower heat, cover, and simmer until beans are tender (about 90 minutes).

2. In a medium skillet over moderate heat, sauté onion in oil until soft; add tomato and sauté until soft. Place ½ cup (125 ml) drained beans in small bowl and mash well with a fork. Add mashed beans to skillet along with ¼ cup (60 ml) of their liquid. Stir over low heat until a thick paste forms.

3. Spoon contents of skillet into bean pot. Simmer, stirring frequently, until liquid thickens (about 30 minutes). Add salt and pepper to taste.

Serves 8.
Each serving: cal 235, fat 4 g, cal from fat 16%, chol 0 mg

Chili Durango

This three-bean chili creates a mosaic of colors and flavors.

1 each	red bell pepper and green bell pepper	1 each
1–2	jalapeño chiles, to taste	1–2
6	fresh Anaheim chiles, roasted (see page 77)	6
	or 1 can (4 oz or 115 g) green chiles	
1½ tbl	olive oil	1½ tbl
2	onions, diced	2
4 cloves	garlic, minced	4 cloves
1 bunch	parsley, finely chopped	1 bunch
2½ cups	small white beans, cooked	600 ml
2½ cups	kidney beans, cooked	600 ml
2½ cups	black beans, cooked	600 ml
8	plum tomatoes, peeled and seeded or	8
	1 can (28 oz or 800 g) crushed plum tomatoes	
4 tsp	salt	4 tsp
1 tsp each	ground cumin and dried oregano	1 tsp each
2 tbl	chili powder	2 tbl
as needed	cilantro (coriander leaves),	as needed
	for garnish	

1. Slice bell peppers in half, remove and discard seeds, and cut into ½-inch (1.25-cm) squares. Mince jalapeños. Cut roasted green chiles in half lengthwise, carefully remove and discard seeds, and chop into ½-inch (1.25-cm) squares.

2. In a saucepan over medium heat, warm the oil and sauté onion for 5 minutes. Add garlic and cook another 1–2 minutes. Stir in peppers, chiles, and parsley. Add cooked beans, tomatoes, salt, cumin, oregano, chili powder, and 2 cups (500 ml) water. Bring to a boil and reduce heat to a simmer; cover and cook 40 minutes more. Serve in shallow bowls with cilantro for garnish.

Serves 8.
Each serving: cal 327, fat 5 g, cal from fat 12%, chol 0 mg

Preparing Roasted Chiles

Chiles contain a substance that can irritate and even severely burn skin and eyes. If you have sensitive skin, wear rubber gloves when handling and peeling chiles. Avoid touching your face, especially your eyes, when working with chiles.

1. *Using tongs, char chiles over a gas flame or electric burner, turning chiles frequently. Do not burn through to the flesh. Place charred chiles in a plastic bag to steam for 10 minutes.*

2. *When chiles are cool, hold them under cool water and carefully peel the chiles, starting from the stem end.*

3. *With a small, sharp knife, cut open the chiles. Remove the veins and seeds and rinse chiles under running water. Blot excess water from chiles. Use at once or wrap in plastic film and freeze.*

CHILI CON CALABAZA

Sugar pumpkins or winter squash can be used in this vegetarian chile.

12	fresh tomatillos, husked and toasted or	12
	2 cans (13 oz or 380 g each) tomatillos	
4	whole poblano chiles, roasted (see page 77) or	
	2 cans (7 oz or 200 g each) poblano chiles	
1	serrano chile	1
2 tbl	olive oil	2 tbl
4 cloves	garlic, diced	4 cloves
2	onions, diced	2
2½ lb	fresh pumpkin or winter squash, peeled seeded, and cubed	1.2 kg
1 tsp each	ground cumin, dried oregano, and salt	1 tsp each
8	plum tomatoes, peeled and seeded or	8
	1 can (28 oz or 800 g) plum tomatoes	
2 cups	corn kernels	500 ml
1½ cups	kidney beans	350 ml
2 tbl	chopped cilantro (coriander leaves), for garnish	2 tbl
¼ cup	green pumpkin seeds, for garnish	60 ml

1. Place tomatillos and chiles in a blender or food processor and purée. Set aside.

2. In a large saucepan over low heat, warm the oil and sauté garlic and onions for 10 minutes. Add pumpkin. Stir in reserved tomatillo-chile sauce, cumin, oregano, and salt. Cook for 20–25 minutes until pumpkin is tender.

3. Drain and quarter tomatoes. Add tomatoes, corn, and kidney beans. Cook for 10 minutes more. Garnish with cilantro and pumpkin seeds.

Serves 8.
Each serving: cal 286, fat 5 g, cal from fat 15%, chol 0 mg

PUMPKIN: FROM SOUP TO NUTS

Cultivated in Mexico since pre-Columbian times, pumpkin (calabaza) can show up almost anywhere in Mexican cuisine. Fresh pumpkin blossoms are a key ingredient in traditional Mexican soups (see Sopa de Flor de Calabaza on page 30); simmered with tomatillos and chiles, pumpkin makes a hearty stew (see Chili con Calabaza on opposite page). Pumpkin purée flavors a number of Mexican custards and sweet breads. Even the seeds (pepitas) of the pumpkin are valued: Hulled and ground into a paste, they are used to thicken the classic cooking sauces known as moles; and roasted and eaten out of hand like peanuts, they make a convenient, nutritious snack.

ELOTES CON QUESO

This classic Mexican treatment for fresh corn adds new interest to a favorite American food. Freshly grated Parmesan or Romano cheese is a good substitute for queso anejo, a sharp, tangy cheese that is seldom available outside Mexico. Dipping the corn in the milk or cream before sprinkling it with the cheese is not essential, but the liquid helps the cheese cling to the corn.

4 ears	corn, husked	4 ears
as needed	milk or light cream (optional)	as needed
4 tbl	freshly grated Parmesan or Romano cheese	4 tbl

1. Place corn in a tightly covered steamer or in a large pot of boiling water. Cook until tender (5–7 minutes).

2. Dip the corn in milk if used, then sprinkle with freshly grated cheese and serve.

Serves 4.
Each serving: cal 66, fat 2 g, cal from fat 26%, chol 4 mg

COLIFLOR ROJO

Although cooked vegetables (verduras) play an important role in Mexican cuisine, unadorned vegetables—except for frijoles—are a rarity. The art of dressing up plain vegetables to create something special is a hallmark of Mexican cooking. This recipe combines two distinctive flavors and colors to transform an ordinary head of cauliflower into a handsome, flavorful side dish.

1 head	cauliflower	1 head
½ recipe	Salsa de Chipotle (see page 18) or bottled salsa	½ recipe
2 tbl	crumbled feta cheese (optional)	2 tbl

1. Break cauliflower into florets. Heat salsa and keep warm.

2. Steam cauliflower until tender (about 9–12 minutes). Do not overcook.

3. Arrange the cauliflower in a serving dish and top with the warm salsa. Garnish with the feta cheese, if used, and serve.

Serves 6.
Each serving: cal 25, fat 1 g, cal from fat 24%, chol 0 mg

DESSERTS AND SWEETS

The delectable Mexican desserts and sweets in this section are all based on fruits, whether churn-frozen into pastel-hued ices vibrant with flavor (see Helados on pages 85–87), still-frozen with spirits into a dessert cocktail (see Margarita Sorbet on page 88), blended into refreshing Mexican-style smoothies (see Licuados on pages 92–94), or composed into a kaleidoscopic still-life of textures, colors, and tastes (see Plato de Frutas on page 90).

Papaya Ice

A refreshing helado (ice) like this one on a hot afternoon or evening offers a pleasant way to cool the body and refresh the spirit. Moist, melon-like papaya makes a particularly delicious helado.

3	fresh papayas, peeled, seeded, and sliced or	3
	2 cans (15 oz or 430 g each) sliced, sweetened papaya	
1 tbl	lime juice (juice of 1 lime)	1 tbl
½ cup	sugar	125 ml

1. Place papaya pieces and lime juice into a blender. Blend to a smooth pulp. If using canned papayas, drain before blending with lime juice, reserving the liquid from the can.

2. Measure the papaya pulp. If using fresh papaya, add water to equal the volume of the fresh pulp. Add sugar and mix well. If using canned papaya, add a combination of the reserved liquid and water to equal the volume of the canned pulp. Add only ¼ cup (60 ml) sugar and mix well.

3. Freeze in an ice cream maker, following the manufacturer's directions (see Homemade Helados on page 86).

4. Serve in chilled serving bowls.

Makes about 4 cups (900 ml), 4 servings.
Each serving: cal 186, fat .3 g, cal from fat 2%, chol 0 mg

STRAWBERRY ICE

Helado de fresca (strawberry ice) captures the intense fragrance, sweet flavor, and appealing color of one of the world's most popular berries (see photo on page 84).

¾ cup	sugar	175 ml
4 cups	strawberries, washed and stemmed	900 ml
1 tbl	lime juice (juice of 1 lime)	1 tbl

1. In a saucepan over medium heat, bring 3 cups (700 ml) of water and sugar to a boil; cook for 5 minutes. Chill syrup. Place strawberries and lime juice into a blender or food processor and purée until smooth.

2. Measure the berry purée and blend with an equal amount of the chilled syrup.

3. Freeze in an ice cream maker, following the manufacturer's directions (see Homemade Helados below).

4. Serve in chilled serving bowls.

Makes about 4 cups (900 ml), 4 servings.
Each serving: cal 191, fat .6 g, cal from fat 3%, chol 0 mg

HOMEMADE HELADOS

Enjoying helados, fine-textured ices made of all manner of fruit, is practically a national pastime in Mexico. Besides familiar flavors like pineapple, orange, and strawberry, Mexican vendors offer cantaloupe, tamarind, mango, papaya, and coconut ices. You can make helados at home, using your favorite fresh, frozen, or canned fruit, and a hand-cranked or electric ice cream freezer. If you use a traditional salt-and-bucket freezer rather than one with a prechilled canister, keep in mind that ices require more rock salt to freeze properly than do ice creams; use about 1¼ parts rock salt to 4 parts ice.

Mango Ice

With a tantalizing perfume and flavor reminiscent of peach, apricot, and papaya, mango makes a delicious helado (ice) (see photo on page 84).

3	fresh mangoes, peeled, seeded, and sliced or	3
	2 cans (15 oz or 430 g each) sliced, sweetened mango	
1 tbl	lime juice (juice of 1 lime)	1 tbl
½ cup	sugar	125 ml

1. Place mango pieces and lime juice into a blender. Blend to a smooth pulp. If using canned mangoes, drain mangoes before blending with lime juice, reserving the liquid from the can.

2. Measure the mango pulp. If using fresh mangoes, add water to equal the volume of the fresh mango pulp. Add sugar and mix well. If using canned papaya, add a combination of the reserved liquid and water to equal the volume of the canned mango pulp. Add only ¼ cup (125 ml) sugar and mix well.

3. Freeze in an ice cream maker, following the manufacturer's directions (see Homemade Helados on page 86).

4. Serve in chilled serving bowls.

Makes about 4 cups (900 ml), 4 servings.
Each serving: cal 198, fat .4 g, cal from fat 2%, chol 0 mg

MARGARITA SORBET

In the dry heat of summer, iced desserts and pick-me-ups—the lighter the better—are especially favored in Mexico. This fluffy sorbet, based on the ingredients of the classic margarita cocktail, is tart enough to serve as a between-course palate refresher; otherwise, it's an adult dessert. You don't need an ice cream freezer to make this sorbet.

1⅛ cups	sugar	280 ml
⅓ cup	lime juice (juice of 4–5 limes)	85 ml
1 tbl	lime pulp (scooped from juiced limes with a teaspoon), seeds removed	1 tbl
2 tbl	gold or añejo tequila	2 tbl
2 tsp	triple sec (citrus liqueur)	2 tsp
2	egg whites	2

1. In a saucepan over medium heat, combine sugar and 2 cups (500 ml) water. Heat until sugar melts and mixture starts to bubble. Cook 10 minutes longer, regulating heat until mixture bubbles gently. Remove from heat and cool slightly.

2. Stir lime juice, lime pulp, tequila, and triple sec into sugar mixture. Pour into a freezerproof serving dish. Still-freeze in freezing compartment of refrigerator until the mixture starts to set (about 1 hour). Remove from freezer and stir briskly with a fork. Return to freezer and chill until mixture is thick and grainy (about 2 more hours), stirring again every half hour or so to keep mixture from freezing solid.

3. Beat egg whites until soft peaks form. Remove mixture from freezer and beat very rapidly to a fluff (using a fork or electric mixer). Immediately fold in egg whites. Return mixture to freezer and chill at least 1 more hour before serving.

Serves 8.
Each serving: cal 129, fat 0 g, cal from fat 0%, chol 0 mg

PLATO DE FRUTAS

This healthy combination of fruits is the typical assortment served as a snack or dessert by the street vendors in Mexico. Although you needn't use all the fruits listed, the greater the variety, the more authentic and tasty the dish will be. The lime and seasonings make a refreshing complement to the sweetness of the fruit. The amount of each fruit you use depends upon your own taste and the availability of the fruits in season.

| 1 each | watermelon, cantaloupe, honeydew melon, mango, papaya, fresh pineapple, jicama, and fresh coconut | 1 each |
| as needed | limes, salt, and ground mild red chiles, for garnish | as needed |

1. Remove seeds and rind from watermelon, cantaloupe, honeydew melon, mango, and papaya; peel pineapple and jicama; crack coconut and peel away brown inner skin. Cut all fruit into bite-sized pieces and mix together.

2. Serve on a large platter with cocktail picks or arrange on individual plates as a first course.

3. Squeeze the fresh limes over the fruit and sprinkle salt and ground chile over the fruit to taste.

The number of servings and nutritional values will depend upon the variety and quantity of fruits used.

Licuado de Melón

Licuados, beverages made by liquefying fresh fruits and other ingredients in a blender, are popular antojitos in Mexico.

| 1 | cantaloupe, watermelon, or honeydew melon | 1 |
| 1 tsp | lime juice | 1 tsp |

Peel and seed melon; cut the melon into chunks. Place approximately 2 cups (500 ml) of melon at a time into a blender or food processor. Blend until liquefied, adding lime juice while blending. Add enough water, about ⅓ cup (85 ml) per 2 cups (500 ml) melon, to blend to a thick liquid. Repeat with remaining melon. Serve chilled.

About four 1-cup (250-ml) servings for a medium-sized cantaloupe.
Each serving: cal 47, fat .4 g, cal from fat 6%, chol 0 mg

Licuado de Fresca

Strawberries make as delicious a licuado as they do a fruit ice (see page 86).

| 4 cups | fresh or frozen strawberries | 900 ml |
| to taste | sugar | to taste |

Wash and stem fresh strawberries. Place strawberries, 2 cups (500 ml) at a time, in a blender or food processor. Add water, about 1–2 cups (250–500 ml) water in all, to blend to a thick liquid. When all the strawberries are blended, check for sweetness and add sugar to taste; blend to mix. Repeat with remaining berries. Serve chilled.

Makes about six 1-cup (250-ml) servings.
Each serving: cal 30, fat .4 g, cal from fat 10%, chol 0 mg

Licuado de Papaya y Naranjas

Papaya and orange are a favorite combination in Mexico. The tartness of the lime juice highlights the sweetness of the other ingredients.

1	ripe papaya	1
1 cup	orange juice	250 ml
1 tsp	lime juice	1 tsp
to taste	sugar	to taste

Peel and seed papaya and cut into chunks. Place in a blender with orange and lime juice. Blend until smooth; taste and add sugar, if necessary. Chill before serving.

Makes two 1-cup (250-ml) servings.
Each serving: cal 116, fat .5 g, cal from fat 3%, chol 0 mg

Licuado de Piña

Pineapple, especially when tree-ripened, is a natural for the Mexican-style smoothie known as a licuado. Mexico exports the Sugar Loaf variety of pineapple, with extra large fruits weighing from 5 to 10 pounds (2.3 to 4.6 kg), to the United States.

| 1 | ripe pineapple, peeled and cut into chunks | 1 |
| ½ cup | sugar | 125 ml |

Place half the pineapple chunks, 2 cups (500 ml) of water, and ¼ cup (60 ml) of the sugar in a blender and blend until smooth. Repeat with the remaining ingredients, adding another 2 cups (500 ml) of water to the mixture. Chill before serving.

Makes about six 1-cup (250-ml) servings.
Each serving: cal 191, fat 1 g, cal from fat 5%, chol 0 mg

INDEX